wedding FLOWERS
IDEAS & INSPIRATION

Talmage McLaurin

Talmage McLaurin is the publisher at Florists' Review
Enterprises, the floral industry's oldest and only independent
publishing house. He has been with the company since 1990.
His floral career began in a family-owned flower business.

Talmage has been a member of the American Institute of
Floral Designers since 1988. He has made six presentations
to the institute at their National Symposiums, and in 2003
he co-chaired the National Symposium, "The Prairie School."
In 2008, Talmage received the AIFD Award of Distinguished
Service to the Floral Industry.

Talmage's trends column and designs appear regularly in
Florists' Review magazine. In addition to this book, his work is
also featured in a number of titles, including _Flower Styling_
(2011), _Sympathy Flowers_ (2011), _Flowers for the Table_ (2010),
Wedding Bouquets (2010), _Ribbons and Flowers_ (2008), _101 How-To_
Favorites Volume 2 (2007), _Flower Arranging_ (2007), _101 Great_
Displays (2005), _Christmas Traditions_ (2004), _Weddings 2_ (2004),
Design School (2003), _101 Wedding Bouquets_ (2002), _Seasons of_
Flowers (2001), _101 How-To Favorites_ (2000), _World Floral Artist 2_
(1999), _Weddings_ (1998), and _Christmas_ (1996).

Refined and rustic elements combine with a wealth

of wildflowers in this floral setting reminiscent of a meadow in bloom.

Untamed Elegance

BOUTONNIERE A pair of hellebores dappled with purple are backed by a pair of dusty miller leaves and a sprig of waxflowers for a just-picked look.

LEFT White lilacs bloom from a base of *Lisianthuses*, hellebores and dusty miller leaves in this hand-tied collection bound with unraveled burlap ribbon and pearl-headed corsage pins.

RIGHT Dainty blooms are arranged into a rustic, diminutive burlap "basket" cleverly created from spray can lids. *See basket how-to on Page 8.*

A textural gathering of hellebores, *Lisianthuses*, lilacs and
Alliums is complemented by the muted gray-green of the
encircling dusty miller leaves. *See collar how-to on Page 8.*

LEAF COLLAR

Cover both sides of a spare ribbon flange or cardboard circle with packing tape for waterproofing and stability.

Coat the backs of dusty miller leaves with spray adhesive.

Press the leaves onto the collar in an overlapping manner.

Insert a foam-cage bouquet holder through the center, and hot-glue the disk to the base of the cage.

POSY BASKET

Secure two spray can lids back to back with adhesive strips. *We used Oasis® UGlu™ Adhesive Strips.*

Wrap the lids with burlap ribbon, and fold over and secure the end with an adhesive strip.

To create a handle, hot-glue a length of cording down each side of the container.

Secure a square of floral foam into the container with hot glue. When ready to arrange, pour water in to soak the foam.

CENTERPIECE Grouped closely on a frayed burlap runner, a trio of arrangements in dark-stained wood containers creates a riot of large- and small-scale blooms that appear to meld into a single composition. 'Attache' roses mingle with the hellebores, *Lisianthuses*, *Alliums*, lilacs, waxflowers and dusty miller.

Bird motifs are an ideal natural touch, from the overt inclusion

of feathers or nests to the subtle use of robin's-egg blue.

Avian Inspiration

BOUTONNIERE A pair of striped feathers is the perfect avian touch to this 'Skyline' rose surrounded with *Berzelia* and dusty miller leaves.

ABOVE Faux eggs nestle among dusty miller leaves in this nest-like collar packed with groups of 'Skyline' roses, 'Renoir' lilies and *Berzelia*. *For collar how-to, see Page 14.*

RIGHT *Hydrangeas* accompany groupings of 'Skyline' roses and *Berzelia* and are balanced by a faux egg-filled nest. *For basket how-to, see Page 14.*

Creamy 'Vendela' roses emerge from amidst
berry-like *Berzelia* and peach stocks interspersed
with eggs and feathers in this muted bouquet.
A feathered hair extension easily elongates
its profile.

FLOWER BASKET

Spray *Hydrangea* blooms with peach-hued floral spray, and slip the flower's stem into a water tube for hydration.

Hot-glue a floral-foam cage into one side of a wicker basket.

Place the *Hydrangeas* into the other side of the basket, hot-gluing the plastic water tube to the wicker.

Arrange elements into the floral foam to fill out the basket, and wrap the basket handle with ribbon, tying bows at each side.

"NEST" COLLAR

Soak angel vine in water to make it pliable, and form it into a circle.

Secure the ends together by wrapping with wire that is covered in brown floral tape.

Insert the wrapped wires through the base of a foam-filled cage, at right angles, and wrap the wire ends around the vine.

Arrange floral materials in groups into the foam, which creates the illusion of a large nest encircling the flowers.

CENTERPIECE Birds perch among the flowering quince branches and nest accents that define this trio of glazed pottery vases. Grouping allows for maximum impact of the 'Renoir' lilies, 'Vendela' roses and carnations. Sprigs of quince flowers and dusty miller accent the trio.

The pansy, a favorite Victorian motif, is accessorized for today with
sumptuous ribbons, "mossed" pots and colorful doilies.

Modern Victorian

BOUTONNIERE One perfect pansy bloom is faced front and center in this simple boutonniere crafted with a trio of blooms and the pansies' foliage.

LEFT Varied purple hues unite in this romantic posy, which uses a halo of carnations to showcase the vivid pansies. Ribbons add a cascading element.

BELOW A mossy basket packed with carnations and pansies – inserted into a small square of glued-in foam – makes a sweet accessory with its ribbon-wrapped handle.

Pansies not only star in this
bouquet of fully opened mini
carnations and 'Little Silver'
mini roses but also form its
luxuriant collar. *See collar
how-to on Page 20.*

19

FAUX MOSS POTS

Put a drop of dishwashing liquid into a spray bottle of water, and liberally spray a terra-cotta pot.

Spray the pot lightly with dark green floral spray and then a generous spray of water. Let set up for 2 to 3 minutes.

Apply a coat of light green floral spray and another layer of water. Wait 2 to 3 minutes.

Spray the final coat, a flat white or white wash floral spray, and a final spray of water. Let the pot dry.

PANSY FLOATING COLLAR

Wrap a wire wreath form with gauzy ribbon to create a base for the blooms.

Insert two heavy-gauge wires at right angles through the base of a foam cage.

Rest the collar atop the wires, and crimp the wires over the edge. Clip the excess wire.

Apply spray adhesive to the backs of pansies, and press them onto the ribbon-covered form.

CENTERPIECE Purple-painted doilies and
faux-moss-covered pots create vintage charm
for an up-to-date setting of small planted
pansies – great favor takeaways – and pansy-
accented carnation orbs. A dot of floral
adhesive on each carnation stem secures the
insertion into the foam sphere, and spray
adhesive holds the pansy blooms on the
carnation surfaces. *See pot how-to at left.*

Sunny daffodils, the herald of spring, are cheery and vibrant

but not too formal for dressing with homespun accessories.

Burst of Sunshine

BOUTONNIERE Snips of grass and mimosa (*Acacia*) accompany a pair of *Ranunculi* tailored with *Ligustrum* leaves as if picked fresh from the garden.

ABOVE The elegant tailoring of this monobotanical bouquet gives it upscale allure, but the yarn-wrapped handle maintains its simple charm. *For handle how-to, see Page 26.*

ABOVE RIGHT Textural tufts of goldenrod (*Solidago*) and mimosa (*Acacia*) contrast the *Lisianthuses* and mini callas in this bridal bouquet, which offers a sunny hint of color.

An asymmetrical gathering of *Ranunculi* and daffodils emerges from a yarn-wrapped disk. The naturally reaching *Ranunculi* stems can be reinforced with wire, if desired. *For collar how-to, see Page 26.*

YARN-WRAPPED COLLAR

Cover both sides of a spare ribbon flange or cardboard circle with packing tape for waterproofing and stability.

Wrap yarn all the way around the circle, at 1-inch intervals, to serve as a guide for the proper radiation.

Wrap the yarn all the way around to fill in the circle, following the angles of the guide lines to keep the wrap even.

Insert a foam-cage bouquet holder through the center, and hot-glue the collar to the base of the cage.

YARN-WRAPPED HANDLE

Gather a bundle of daffodils so that the blooms naturally form a half-moon nosegay shape.

Bind the stem bundle at the top and bottom with waterproof tape, to keep the stems from twisting.

Wrap acrylic yarn – which will wick less moisture – closely around the stems, covering both bands of tape.

Insert a vertical row of pearl-headed corsage pins, or other jeweled pins, for a tailored finish.

26

CENTERPIECE Daffodils emerge from thick carpets of grass in a brilliant show of spring. Water picks hydrate the flowers and are inserted into the pet grass, which serves as a ready-made accent. Yarn-wrapped vine balls complete the setting.

27

From monarch markings to filigreed damask to spiraling

Echeveria leaves, distinctive patterns define this floral setting.

Bohemian Butterflies

BOUTONNIERE Butterfly wings replace the traditional foliage accompanying a single 'Sweetness' rose. Tiny *Echeveria* sprigs add a hint of green.

LEFT A dazzling filigree-patterned handle adorns an eclectic collection of 'Sweetness' and 'Art Deco' roses, tulips, *Echeverias* and statice. The bicolored roses and *Hoya* leaves mirror the swirling patterns.

RIGHT The distinctive pattern of the monarch wing is refashioned into a chic, one-of-a-kind ring pillow adorned with tiny *Echeverias* and a few intact butterflies that appear to have alighted for a brief respite. *See pillow how-to on Page 32.*

The graphic markings of the hot pink monarch
butterfly wings set off a rich collection of
'Sweetness' and 'Art Deco' roses, mini callas,
and *Echeverias*. *See collar how-to on Page 32.*

BUTTERFLY COLLAR

Spray adhesive over the top of a woven doll hat.

Press the bouquet holder through the center of the hat dome and into the brim.

Using wire cutters, clip the faux butterfly wings from the bodies.

Spray adhesive onto wing backs, and press around the brim to create a patterned edge.

BUTTERFLY PILLOW

Using wire cutters, clip the faux butterfly wings from the bodies.

Spray the backs of the wings with adhesive, and press onto the top of the pillow.

Affix several intact butterflies atop the pillow with adhesive strips. *We used Oasis® UGlu™ Adhesive Dashes.*

Add small clusters of *Echeveria* with waterproof adhesive.

CENTERPIECE Black and white floral damask offers an arresting yet neutral backdrop for the patterned and textural blooms in these compact arrangements of 'Shocking' lilies, 'Sweetness' and 'Art Deco' roses, statice, *Echeverias* and *Hoya* leaves.

Raw wood and other humble materials combine with deep green floral

elements to communicate a reverence for Mother Earth.

Sustainable Chic

BOUTONNIERE *Ligustrum* leaves surround a cluster of *Hypericum* berries from which the foliage has been stripped.

ABOVE A variegated lily grass mat covers a standard ring pillow, its lace edging removed. Fine-gauge wire secures the egg-filled nest, *Hydrangea* sprigs and *Hypericum* berry bow for added stability. *See weaving how-to on Page 38.*

LEFT Clusters of *Hydrangeas* just opening into bloom are gathered with a rustic burlap ribbon secured with gunmetal-colored corsage pins.

Mossy *Dianthuses* encircle 'White
O'Hara' roses while a pearl-like
garland of green *Hypericum* berries
adds an elegant but natural touch.
See bow how-to on Page 38.

WOVEN RING PILLOW

Align enough lily grass blades side by side to more than cover the width of a pillow, and tape down one end.

Weave lily grass into the taped-down blades, alternating over and under the blades. Slide the blades close together.

When the appropriate size square is reached, cover the blades with clear packing tape to hold the shape.

Flip the mat, so the tape is on the bottom, and trim edges to desired size. Affix to pillow with low-temperature glue.

HYPERICUM BOW

Remove *Hypericum* berries from their branches.

String berries onto flexible, fine-gauge beading wire.

Form the berry garland into a bow shape.

Wrap a wired wood pick around the center of the bow for easy insertion into the bouquet holder.

CENTERPIECE Monobotanical bouquets of *Hydrangeas*, carnations, spider chrysanthemums and *Dianthuses* are displayed in natural wood boxes, and other wooden accents – including oversized table numbers – keep the look clean and "green."

The lavender flower, with its fragrant buds and romantic hue,

inspires a floral setting with a quaint country aesthetic.

Lavender Love

BOUTONNIERE A tight wrapping of purple aluminum wire gathers a fragrant cluster of flowering lavender.

ABOVE 'Cool Water' roses, chrysanthemums, *Lisianthuses* and lavender overflow from a petite woven purse accented with burlap-backed wire leaves and a fresh striped bow. *For leaf how-to, see Page 44.*

LEFT A swirling collar of frayed burlap ribbon, along with the ribbons' detached wired edges and knotted satin ribbon, adds a deconstructed beauty to this collection of chrysanthemums and seeded *Eucalyptus* and also protects the edges of the delicate blooms.

High-style 'Cool Water' roses take on a more rustic charm with the addition of burlap-backed wire leaves and a burlap collar and ribbon tails. *For how-to, see Page 44.*

WIRE HEARTS AND LEAVES

BURLAP COLLAR

Form a heart and leaves on a strand of aluminum wire with needle-nosed pliers. A cookie cutter provides a template.

Cover both sides of a spare ribbon flange or cardboard circle with packing tape to waterproof and stabilize.

Affix the shaped wire to a burlap ribbon with spray adhesive, spraying the wire only.

Press burlap ribbon, with the wire edge removed, onto the circle with spray adhesive.

When the adhesive is dry, trim around the wire shapes to remove the excess ribbon.

Trim the burlap from the center and edges, and hot-glue a bouquet holder into the center of the collar.

CENTERPIECE Simple and unfussy, these canning jars are decorated with burlap-backed hearts and leaves and hold a wild assortment of 'Cool Water' roses, chrysanthemums, *Trachelium* and lavender. Sweet gum balls add to the fresh-plucked ambiance of the textural florals. *See how-to at left.*

Wrap the extra length of the wire around the lip of a canning jar, and spiral the end for a rustic accent.

Insert burlap-backed wire leaves into the bouquet in place of foliage, and add burlap ribbon tails to finish.

Luscious sorbet-colored garden roses take on a formal but feminine

air when paired with classic pottery and trailing ivy.

Southern Belle

BOUTONNIERE Two types of leaves – rose and lamb's ear – frame a single 'Miranda' garden rose.

ABOVE This treasure from the garden mixes a variety of "roses." Garden roses 'Patience', 'Miranda' and 'Juliet' are joined by Lenten roses (hellebores) in a collar of lamb's ears. *For collar how-to, see Page 50.*

LEFT A stunning composite lily improves upon nature by multiplying the gorgeous petals. Tendrils of ivy add a natural cascade. *For lily how-to, see Page 50.*

Ivy creates both the collar and cascade for this bouquet of 'Patience', 'Miranda' and 'Juliet' garden roses.

COMPOSITE LILY

Remove the pistil and stamen from the center of a lily. Wire and tape a lily bud, and insert it into the center.

To hold the "flower" together, wire horizontally through the petals and the bud, folding and taping these wires down.

Squeeze floral adhesive in lines onto lily petals, and press the petals onto a flange to cover it.

Glue the new wired lily "flower" into the center of the petal-covered flange to create an oversized bloom.

LAMB'S EAR COLLAR

Cover both sides of a spare ribbon flange or cardboard circle with packing tape to waterproof and stabilize.

Coat the backs of lamb's ear leaves with spray adhesive.

Place the leaves in an over-lapping pattern onto the circle, folding the leaves over the outer edge.

Secure the collar onto a floral-foam-filled bouquet holder with hot glue.

CENTERPIECE All-white urns offer a traditional backdrop for
lush collections of lilies, garden roses – 'Patience', 'Miranda'
and 'Juliet' – and *Hypericum* berries. Simple drapes of ivy
complete the tableau.

Citrus-inspired chartreuse is a fresh foil for classic blue delft

patterns, offering a cool, modern twist on a classic motif.

Twist of Lime

BOUTONNIERE Sleek spiraling tendrils and leaves of aluminum wire – surrounding a sprig of *Hypericum* berries – are a stylish make-ahead alternative for a lapel.

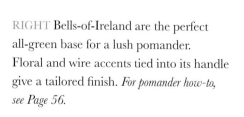

LEFT A modern monobotanical bouquet of *Cymbidium* orchids has a sculptural setting in this collar of aluminum wire foliage. *For collar how-to, see Page 56.*

RIGHT Bells-of-Ireland are the perfect all-green base for a lush pomander. Floral and wire accents tied into its handle give a tailored finish. *For pomander how-to, see Page 56.*

Leaf-like *Cymbidium* orchid petals
mirror the *Camellia* leaves in this
grouped bouquet that also features
Hydrangeas and *Hypericum* berries.

POMANDER

Loop one end of a heavy-gauge wire, and pierce through the center of a floral foam sphere soaked in flower-food solution.

With the wire loop abutting the sphere, wind the wire "tail" around a wood pick to hold the wire securely in the sphere.

Snip bells-of-Ireland into segments. Dip the stems into waterproof floral adhesive, and insert them into the foam.

Tie a ribbon-loop handle onto the wire loop, which keeps the ribbon elevated so it won't wick moisture from the sphere.

WIRE LEAF COLLAR

Form the end of a length of aluminum wire into two leaves, shaping the leaf tips with a pair of needle-nosed pliers.

Create two leaves at the other end of the wire, and fold the wire in half. Create a few more of these wire leaf pairs.

Gather the pairs and, using a pencil, twist the wires to form a handle as the leaf cluster is held secure with pliers.

Fan the leaves into a collar shape. Place a group of wired and taped orchids atop the collar, and tape onto the handle.

CENTERPIECE Dainty delft cachepots in a variety of patterns make a one-of-a-kind composite arrangement that is punctuated with the cheery hues of the 'Super Green' roses and fresh limes – both whole and sliced. *Hydrangeas*, *Hypericum* berries and *Camellia* leaves are grouped alongside these elements.

A wealth of eye-catching patterns and a rainbow of colors enhance the

cheery and lighthearted tone of graphic Gerberas.

BOUTONNIERE A single hot-pink mini *Gerbera* makes a bold statement backed with a trio of *Ligustrum* leaves.

ABOVE Folded *Ligustrum* leaves give a delicate, pleated finish to this basket, which contains a small square of foam glued inside to hydrate the mini *Gerberas*. *See basket how-to on Page 62.*

LEFT The vivid colors in this hand-tied gathering of mini *Gerberas* are complemented by the bright teal ribbon tie and jewel-toned corsage pins.

White and yellow mini *Gerberas* are interspersed in
a base of white *Hydrangeas* and finished with a
candy-color striped bow for a cheery bouquet.

LEAF BASKET

Place adhesive strips vertically to cover a waterproof plastic container. *We used Oasis® UGlu™ Adhesive Strips.*

Group several lily grass stems, and press the ends onto the adhesive on either side of the pot to create a handle.

Fold *Ligustrum* leaves in half lengthwise and press the spines onto the adhesive, placing them closely together.

Trim the bottoms of the *Ligustrum* leaves flush with the bottom of the pot.

FABRIC-COVERED BOX

Trace a box in the center of the back side of a fabric square cut long enough to fold over the box top.

Trim out the corners to create four flaps. One pair should be equal in width to the box's sides, the other pair slightly wider.

Spray the flaps with adhesive. Fold the two wider flaps up and press onto the box, into the interior and around the sides.

Fold the remaining flaps up and onto the box, pressing the top of the fabric into the box's interior.

CENTERPIECE Patterned fabrics cover paper boxes, offering
an infinite variety of custom looks. Geometric patterns and
bold blooms create a charming contrast with the more refined
patterns of the cups and saucers. *See how-to at left.*

Treasures from the sea accompany flowers in a muted color palette

of gold, peach and cream for a warm seaside ambiance.

Sand and Surf

BOUTONNIERE A ring of billy buttons (*Craspedia*) and *Hypericum* berries encircle the base of a 'Cinnamon' rose, which is backed with *Hypericum* leaves.

ABOVE Ribbon-like variegated *Aspidistra* leaves provide a sleek, visual backing to *Phalaenopsis* orchids, *Leucospermums* and callas in this tropical cascade.

RIGHTY A dainty, bow-tied Nantucket basket is ringed with seashells and mirrors the assortment from the attendant's bouquet. *For seashell how-to, see Page 68.*

Sunny and sandy hues combine in this textural grouping of billy buttons (*Craspedia*), *Hypericum* berries, and 'Cinnamon' and 'Gipsy Curiosa' roses. *For bamboo handle how-to, see Page 68.*

67

SEASHELL ACCENTS

Carefully drill holes into centers of seashells with a small drill bit.

Form a tight spiral in one end of a length of aluminum wire. Thread through a shell, keeping the spiral on the outside.

Secure a floral-foam-filled cage into the basket with hot glue.

Insert the seashells into the foam, arranging them horizontally around the basket.

BAMBOO BOUQUET HANDLE

Using a small saw, trim bamboo to the desired bouquet handle length.

Clip the bouquet holder handle short so it will fit into the bamboo, which is sectioned off by solid nodes.

Wrap the base of the plastic bouquet holder with florists' clay.

Press the holder into the bamboo. For added stability, drill through the bamboo and plastic base and secure with wire.

CENTERPIECE The starfish – arranged first in this trio of cubes –
serve both as key visual elements as well as a brace for the expressive
Leucospermums, parrot tulips, billy buttons (*Craspedia*) and *Hypericum* berries,
which are arranged in a single direction to maintain the view into the cubes.

*Classic patterns and fun accents add a dapper and delightful look to
the contemporary complements of hot pink and lime green.*

Wild and Whimsical

BOUTONNIERE A lime-green houndstooth fabric, covering silk corsage leaves, adds style to a traditional single-bloom boutonniere.

ABOVE Whimsical green butterflies alight atop pink parrot tulips accented by a fashionable handle cover with houndstooth ribbon tails.

LEFT A 3D effect is created on this carnation pomander with the strategically placed *Ligustrum* leaves, which highlight a central tuft of blooms and a colorful butterfly.

In this colorful twist on a classic round bouquet, 'Attache' roses are surrounded by a collar of layered petals and glossy *Ligustrum* leaves. *See collar how-to on Page 74.*

PETAL COLLAR

Cover both sides of a spare ribbon flange or cardboard circle with packing tape to waterproof and stabilize.

Cover the surface with spray adhesive and wait a few seconds for it to become tacky.

Press the edges of the rose petals onto the collar, overlapping in concentric circles.

Insert a foam-cage bouquet holder through the center, and hot-glue the disk to the base of the cage.

TOPIARY BASE

Secure a block of floral foam into a terra-cotta pot with pan-melt glue.

Strip the leaves from leftover rose stems, and trim the stems to roughly equal lengths.

Press the stems into the foam, aligning them closely together around the edge of the pot.

Insert a bouquet holder into the center of the pot. The stems will conceal it. Arrange flowers into the foam cage.

CENTERPIECE A wealth of hot-pink florals – 'Attache' roses, parrot tulips, carnations and mini *Gerberas* – is accented with green *Hypericum* berries and silk butterflies in these faux topiaries. *See topiary base how-to at left.*

75

From sunny gold to deep amber, a range of orange hues unites in this

fresh collection inspired by the dainty clementine.

Oranges Grove

BOUTONNIERE **A few** *Stephanotises* **and** *Camellia* **leaves are tied with satin ribbon for a casual but elegant boutonniere.**

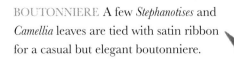

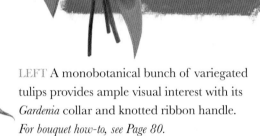

LEFT **A monobotanical bunch of variegated tulips provides ample visual interest with its** *Gardenia* **collar and knotted ribbon handle.** *For bouquet how-to, see Page 80.*

ABOVE **What appears to be a pavéd basket of intact tulips is actually a cleverly created mass of petals for tossing.** *For basket how-to, see Page 80.*

Citrus-hued 'Mango' callas, roses, and *Gerberas* intermingle with *Stephanotises* and *Camellia* leaves in a silk-covered bouquet handle.

RIBBON-TIED BOUQUET

Remove tulip leaves and clean the stems with a floral knife to strip off the "brackets" where the foliage is attached.

After clustering tulips into a nosegay shape, add *Gardenia* foliage around the edge to protect and collar the blooms.

Bind the stem bundle at the top and bottom with waterproof tape to prevent twisting.

Knot short lengths of ribbon around the handle, sliding the knots close together to cover the stems.

LEAF-COVERED BASKET

Using spray adhesive, layer *Camellia* leaves to cover a cardboard box.

Affix a length of ribbon on either side of the basket with adhesive strips to form a handle. *We used Oasis® UGlu™ Adhesive Strips.*

Create two simple Dior bows and press them onto the sides of the basket with adhesive. *We used Oasis® UGlu™ Adhesive Dashes.*

Hold the tops of yet-to-open tulips, snip off their bases and wedge them in the basket for ready-to-toss petals.

CENTERPIECE The vivid orange of the clementines massed in glass urns and picked into glazed orange pottery is broken only by the *Camellia* leaves and *Stephanotises* radiating from the arrangements. The delicate blooms are taped to *Stephanotis* stems for hydration and stability.

Glittering costume jewelry — whether heirloom or newly discovered —

pairs perfectly with jewel-toned blooms in an opulent array.

Something Borrowed

BOUTONNIERE A single enameled flower is surrounded by leaflike jewel clusters and silken corsage leaves for an everlasting accompaniment.

ABOVE This dainty tussy-mussy incorporates a variety of flower-shaped brooches among a gathering of faux leaves and velvet ribbon roses.

LEFT Four colors of callas complement the hues in the distinctive, heart-shaped brooch that decorates the velvet-ribbon-wrapped stems.

A glittering array of multi-colored brooches is a fashion-forward yet personal way to incorporate classic elements with modern sophistication. Gather costume jewelry from personal collections or pick it up at flea markets and garage sales. Even broken pieces can be used, because the imperfect parts can be layered beneath other brooches. *For brooch how-to, see Page 86.*

BROOCH BOUQUET

Flatten two wire collars, and press one atop the other for a denser surface. Secure together with a few small wires.

Form the malleable wire into a dome shape, which will become the outline for the bouquet.

Fold long, sturdy-gauge wires into hairpin shapes. Push the wire ends through the center of the mesh to create a handle.

Slide the loose wires through a third wire collar, scrunching it up to form a handle. Wire brooches onto the dome.

BANDED BOXES

Fold ribbon – cut to a length just shorter than the perimeter of the container – into thirds. Adhesive dashes secure the fold.

Crimp the ends of the ribbon and cinch them with wire to give a puckered effect.

Wrap the ribbon around the middle of the container, using adhesive dashes to hold it in place.

Attach a brooch to the container with an adhesive dash, covering the ribbon ends for a buckle-like appearance.

CENTERPIECE The deep rouge callas and pastel pink 'Sorbonne' lilies mirror the hues in the velvety ribbons and enameled brooches that adorn these black containers. Mini *Cymbidium* orchids and *Galax* and begonia leaves add more touches of color, and oversized jewels shimmer on the tabletop. *See container how-to at left.*

Orchids add an exotic aura to any setting, and here the glamour

is amped up with vibrant colors, shimmer and sheen.

Uptown Orchids

BOUTONNIERE Wire wrapped in floral tape and fuchsia ribbon is formed into a modern loop and spiral pattern to accent a single *Phalaenopsis* orchid.

ABOVE A foliage-free cluster of *Phalaenopsis* orchids rests on a cushion of rumpled ribbons, inspiring interest with varied textures and patterns. *For ruffled holder how-to, see Page 92.*

LEFT A *Trachelium* nosegay base provides a subtle green backdrop for a cascade of white *Phalaenopsis* orchids.

Individual orchid blooms are inserted into water tubes concealed within this cloud of tree fern. A coordinating fuchsia ribbon wrap embellished with jeweled ribbon mirrors the orchids' vivid hue.

For fern collar how-to, see Page 92.

TREE FERN COLLAR

Gather about one and a half bunches of tree fern, and wrap the stem bundle at the top and bottom with waterproof tape.

Press the fronds straight down onto the table – they will fan into a circle – and trim the ends into a neat circle.

Lift the fronds off the table, fluff them out and trim the pouf into a nosegay shape.

Glue water picks with floral adhesive into the fronds to hold the orchid stems.

RUFFLED BOUQUET HOLDER

Insert a water tube into the center of a premade bouquet handle cover with a drop of pan-melt glue to secure it.

Create a multi-loop bow, and secure it with a floral tie. *We used the Wrapsit Floral Tie from Syndicate Sales.*

Insert the end of the floral tie into the foam of the handle cover, fluff the loops and pin them in place with corsage pins.

Insert the *Phalaenopsis* orchid stems into the water tube.

CENTERPIECE Glass candleholders elevate all-white orchid spheres from which gorgeous waves of fuchsia *Phalaenopsis* orchids cascade. Iridescent ornaments add to the modern fantasy setting. Insert the orchids at the last minute for maximum freshness.

Vivid complements of orange and blue inspire this distinctive mix

of flowers and foliage that can cross from spring to fall.

Something Blue

BOUTONNIERE Two folded *Magnolia* leaves – the first stapled and the second glued to the first – create a pocket for a tuft of *Eryngium* blossoms.

LEFT A whimsical mix of wire leaves, gauzy ribbon and a *Hydrangea*-covered collar add contemporary flair to 'Royal Sunset' lilies, *Cymbidium* orchids, *Eryngiums* and *Hydrangeas*.

RIGHT A sea of *Hydrangea* blossoms washes over this ring pillow. The lace trim has been removed, and floral adhesive holds the blossoms in place.

'Royal Sunset' lilies, 'Leonitas' roses, *Eryngiums*, hyacinths and *Hydrangeas* present a complementary color palette atop a collar of russet-colored *Magnolia* leaves. *For collar how-to, see Page 98.*

MAGNOLIA LEAF COLLAR

Snip V-shaped segments from *Magnolia* leaves, and glue them against a bouquet holder handle so that the backsides face out.

Fold a *Magnolia* leaf in half, top-side together, and staple to hold it secure.

Cut off the tapered bottom of the folded leaf, and slide the leaf over the handle, securing it with floral adhesive.

Repeat Steps 2 and 3, sliding these leaves onto the bouquet handle in alternating directions for a skirted effect.

LEAF-COVERED VASE

Place a rubber band around an upside-down cylinder vase, and slide *Magnolia* leaves under the band, backsides facing out.

Continue sliding leaves under the rubber band, overlapping them to cover the entire vase.

Cut *Magnolia* leaves in half, and place a line of glue along the cut edges to adhere to the base of the vase.

Glue these leaf halves around the base of the vase, covering the rubber band and any bare glass.

CENTERPIECE A leaf-covered vase filled with gold- and blue-hued blooms of 'Royal Sunset' lilies, *Hydrangeas* and hyacinths is accompanied by a few *Magnolia* leaves and a ribbon-tied bunch of hyacinths. The bold color combo lends itself either to spring – in which it serves as a contrast to the usual pastels of the season – or to fall – when forced hyacinths allow for the same floral selection. *See vase how-to at left.*

Simple elements create a rich fall palette. The deep rust tones of turning leaves play alongside pine cones and creamy roses.

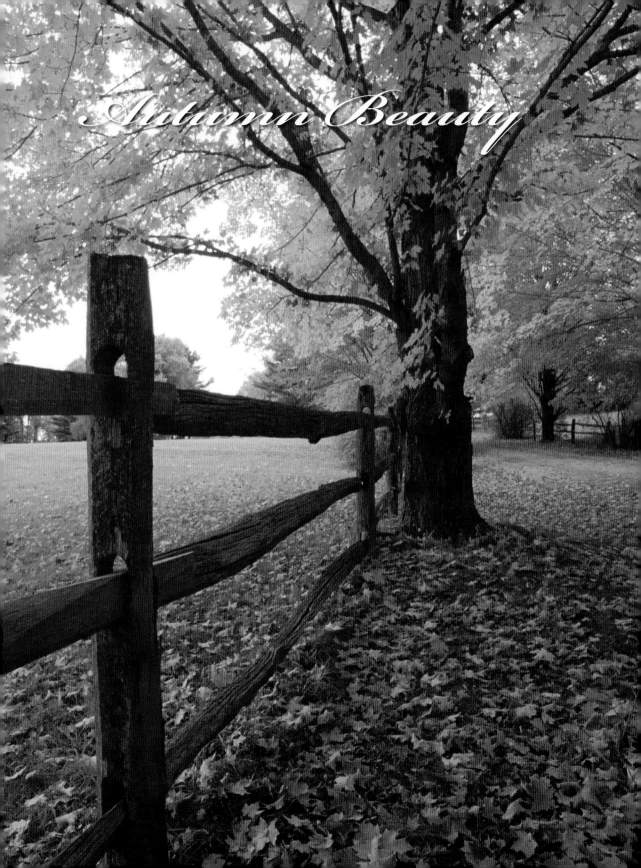

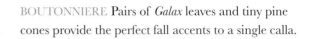

BOUTONNIERE Pairs of *Galax* leaves and tiny pine cones provide the perfect fall accents to a single calla.

ABOVE This composite, or duchess, rose creates a stunning oversized presence for a 'Caramel Antike' bloom. A multi-layered collar of rose petals surrounds the single rose, while *Galax* leaves provide a verdant backing. *For a similar fantasy flower how-to, see Page 50.*

LEFT Glossy, deep-hued callas offer a unique collar for a collection of roses and tiny pine cones. The callas' central spadices are removed and the petals flattened before insertion into the bouquet holder. *For handle how-to, see Page 104.*

Hypericum berries and button spray chrysanthemums provide a dainty, jewel-like accompaniment to this rose bouquet, which is set atop a *Galax* leaf collar.

GALAX-COVERED CUBE

Trim the stems from a bunch of *Galax* leaves.

Spray the backs of the leaves with floral adhesive.

Press the leaves onto the cube container, starting at the top and layering the leaves to cover it.

Trim the leaves flush with the base of the cube.

SLIP-ON HANDLE

Cut a tapered cone of dry foam slightly longer than the handle of the bouquet holder.

Use a small block of foam like sandpaper to shape the foam cone into a smooth taper.

Dip the bouquet holder handle into pan-melt glue, and press it into the center of the foam cone.

Coat the backs of *Galax* leaves with spray adhesive, and layer them onto the cone to cover it.

CENTERPIECE Callas intersperse with golden-hued roses in a trio of *Galax*-covered cubes for a simple but stunning fall display. Luxurious ribbon and pine cones provide a tabletop accent. *See cube how-to at left.*

Deep mauve and burgundy blooms and exotic patterns mingle with sparkling

silver and rich black for a wild, opulent and fashion-forward mix.

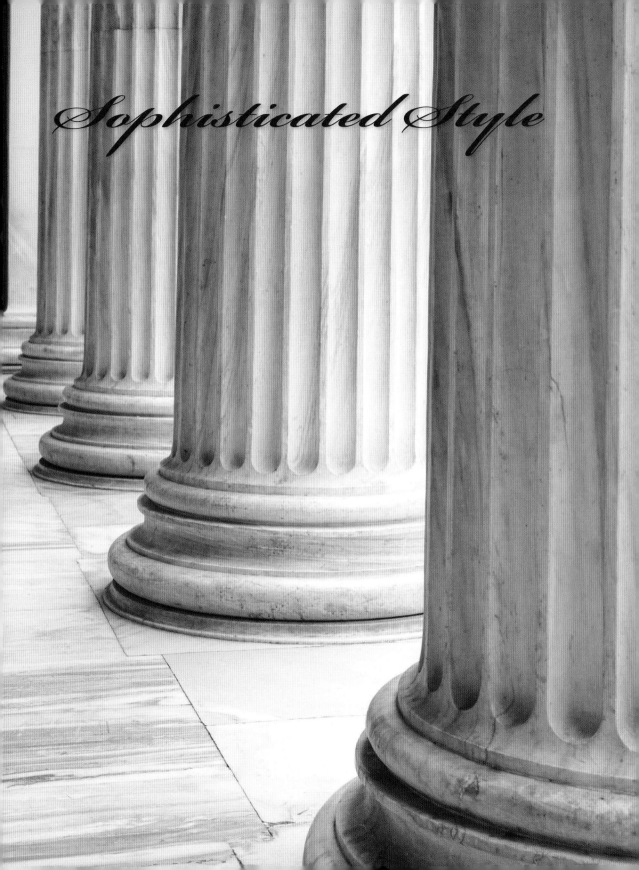

Sophisticated Style

BOUTONNIERE A pair of fern fronds playfully accents a pair of 'Red Vission' roses.

ABOVE A flower-festooned beaded purse is a fun and easy-to-carry accent for maids or mothers. Water tubes hold the *Cymbidium* orchid, roses and *Camellia* leaves.

LEFT The glossy sheen of 'Dark Schwarzwalder' callas nearly passes for black, making this monobotanical bouquet a stunning option. Silver ribbon and corsage pins contrast nicely at the handle.

Glossy, deep-burgundy peonies join 'Red
Vission' roses on a bejeweled, python-pat-
terned bouquet collar for a high-fashion,
foliage-free look. The fern fronds' natural
curls and jet hue add a playful mystique.
For collar how-to, see Page 110.

PYTHON-PRINT COLLAR

Trace a ribbon flange onto foam-centered board, and cut it out to create a collar form.

Spray the collar with adhesive, and cover with fabric. Trim excess fabric.

Insert pearl-headed corsage pins horizontally around the edge of the collar.

Insert a foam-cage bouquet holder through the center, and hot-glue the collar to the base of the cage.

FLOWER PEDESTAL

Cut a cube of floral foam to fit a square plastic tray. Place the soaked foam atop the tray.

Insert carnations at the four corners of the base, with drops of floral adhesive, and then fill in between the corners.

Continue creating rows of carnations, starting at the corners and filling in between, to cover the sides of the cube.

Secure the plastic tray to a candlestick with florists' clay, and place flowers into the top of the floral foam.

CENTERPIECE *Cymbidium* orchids, *Camellia* leaves and fern fronds erupt from carnation-covered bases in these floral twists on the traditional topiary. Candlesticks, which can be painted to match, make simple stands. The *Camellia* leaves offer a quick and natural table scatter option. *See pedestal how-to at left.*

Layered red hues add youthful energy while seasonal accessories keep

this classic red and white pairing warm and nostalgic.

Winter's Kiss

BOUTONNIERE Red jingle bells of varying sizes join a quartet of wool-covered corsage leaves to highlight a single 'Pink Piano' garden rose. *See leaf how-to on Page 116.*

ABOVE Pure as new-fallen snow, 'White O'Hara' roses are accented with a downy, large-scale woolen bow made all the more lush with the fabric folded into thirds.

LEFT Corsage leaves – some cleverly coordinated in red wool – surround garden roses in a range of blushing hues. A few roses still in bud stage offer a verdant complement. *See leaf how-to on Page 116.*

'Best Impression', 'Pink Piano' and 'Red Piano' garden roses create a luscious, candy-colored mix offset by a velvet bow and a wool collar. *See collar how-to on Page 116.*

WOOL-COVERED LEAVES

Coat tops of satin corsage leaves with spray adhesive. Wait 30 seconds, until tacky.

Press a strip of wool onto the leaves, and let the adhesive set.

Trim around the outlines of the leaves, leaving the stems attached.

For additional accents, string jingle bells of varied sizes onto thin wire wrapped in red floral tape.

FLOATING WOOL COLLAR

Wrap a strip of wool – folded into thirds along its length – onto a wire wreath form.

Once the wreath form is encircled, secure the overlapping edges with hot glue.

Wrap two heavy-gauge wires with red floral tape, and insert them, at right angles, through the base of a foam cage.

Rest the collar atop the wires, and crimp the wires over the top, clipping off the excess wire.

LOCATIONS:

St. Louis, MO
(Headquarters)
800-264-4617

Quincy, IL
800-738-8256

Cape Girardeau, MO
800-960-0270

Kansas City, MO
888-859-4199

Springfield, MO
866-832-8977

Topeka, KS
800-523-0013

Wichita, KS
800-362-2635

Phoenix, AZ
602-285-0888

SINCE 1952

Baisch & Skinner
WHOLESALE FLORAL DISTRIBUTOR
WWW.BAISCHANDSKINNER.COM

Your Leading Wholesale Floral Supplier for Everything- Wedding!

- Fresh Flowers
- Greenery
- Glassware
- Ribbon
- Decorative Accessories
- Floral Supplies
- Permanent Botanicals

FLORISTS' REVIEW

President: Frances Dudley, AAF
Publisher: Talmage McLaurin, AIFD
Floral Designer: Talmage McLaurin, AIFD
Author: Amy Bauer
Art Director: Linda Park
Graphic Editor: Holly Cott
Title and Cover Art: John Collins
Copy Editors: Shelley Urban, Kelsey Smith
Photographer: John Collins

Wedding Flowers: Ideas & Inspiration
was produced by Florists' Review Enterprises, Inc.,
Topeka, Kansas; www.floristsreview.com.

Printed in China
ISBN: 978-0-9854743-0-0

Florists' Review Enterprises is the leading magazine and book
publishing company for the U.S. floral industry. The company
is home to *Florists' Review* and *Super Floral Retailing* magazines as
well as to Florists' Review Bookstore, the industry's premier
marketplace for books and other educational materials.